EMMANUEL JOSEPH

The Philosopher's Code, Unlocking the Intersection of History and Technology

Copyright © 2025 by Emmanuel Joseph

All rights reserved. No part of this publication may be reproduced, stored or transmitted in any form or by any means, electronic, mechanical, photocopying, recording, scanning, or otherwise without written permission from the publisher. It is illegal to copy this book, post it to a website, or distribute it by any other means without permission.

First edition

*This book was professionally typeset on Reedsy.
Find out more at reedsy.com*

Contents

1	Chapter 1: Bridging Two Worlds	1
2	Chapter 2: The Dawn of Philosophy: Ancient Wisdom	3
3	Chapter 3: Renaissance Rebirth: The Age of Enlightenment	5
4	Chapter 4: Industrial Revolution: The Steam-Powered Paradigm...	7
5	Chapter 5: Early Twentieth Century: Technological Genesis	9
6	Chapter 6: The Digital Frontier: Silicon Valley and Beyond	11
7	Chapter 7: Artificial Intelligence: Conscious Machines?	13
8	Chapter 8: Cyber Ethics: Technology and Morality	15
9	Chapter 9: The Knowledge Paradox: Information Overload	17
10	Chapter 10: Modern Philosophy: Reinterpreting Classical...	19
11	Chapter 11: Technological Determinism: Shaping Society	21
12	Chapter 12: Future Visions: The Singularity	23
13	Chapter 13: Augmented Reality: Blending Realms	25
14	Chapter 14: Sustainable Tech: Green Philosophies	27
15	Chapter 15: Conclusion: The Ever-Evolving Intersection	29

1

Chapter 1: Bridging Two Worlds

Throughout human history, the interplay between philosophical thought and technological advancement has shaped our civilizations in profound ways. While philosophy sought to understand the deeper meanings of life, existence, and ethics, technology aimed to improve the quality of that very existence. The balance and tension between these two domains have resulted in a dynamic, ever-evolving narrative that has driven humanity forward. This book aims to explore the critical junctures where philosophy and technology have intersected, and how they have collectively molded the world we live in today.

The roots of this fascinating convergence can be traced back to the earliest days of human civilization. Ancient philosophers like Socrates, Plato, and Aristotle pondered the fundamental questions of human existence while observing and theorizing about the natural world around them. Concurrently, early technological innovations—such as the wheel, fire, and simple tools—began to shape human society in practical ways. The connection between abstract thought and tangible invention was already evident, suggesting that the progress of humanity relied on a blend of intellectual and material advancements.

As centuries passed, this relationship between philosophy and technology grew increasingly intricate. The Renaissance, an era of profound cultural, artistic, and scientific rejuvenation, witnessed philosophers and inventors collaborating more than ever before. Figures like Leonardo da Vinci and Galileo Galilei epitomized the fusion of philosophical inquiry and technological innovation, pushing the boundaries of what was known and possible. This chapter will delve into the early intersections of these fields and set the stage for an exploration of how they have continued to influence each other throughout history.

In examining the role of philosophy and technology, it becomes clear that neither can exist in isolation. Philosophy provides the ethical framework and critical thinking necessary to guide technological progress, while technology offers new tools and methodologies for philosophical exploration. This symbiotic relationship has driven humanity to unimaginable heights, and as we stand on the precipice of an even more technologically advanced future, understanding this interplay becomes all the more crucial. This book will serve as a guide to navigating the complexities of this intersection, offering insights into how we can harness the power of both to shape a better world.

2

Chapter 2: The Dawn of Philosophy: Ancient Wisdom

The origins of philosophical thought are deeply rooted in the ancient civilizations of Greece, China, and India. These early thinkers were less concerned with the practical applications of technology and more focused on understanding the nature of reality, existence, and human behavior. In Greece, figures like Thales, Pythagoras, and Heraclitus laid the groundwork for Western philosophy with their explorations of metaphysics, mathematics, and the cosmos. Their inquiries were often driven by a sense of wonder and curiosity about the natural world, setting the stage for future philosophical and scientific endeavors.

In ancient China, philosophers like Confucius and Laozi approached these questions from a different perspective, emphasizing ethics, governance, and the harmony between humanity and nature. Confucius' teachings on moral conduct, social relationships, and statecraft provided a philosophical framework that influenced Chinese society for centuries. Meanwhile, Laozi's Taoism offered a more mystical approach, advocating for a life of simplicity and alignment with the natural order. These Eastern philosophies, though distinct from their Western counterparts, similarly sought to understand the human condition and the principles underlying the universe.

India's ancient philosophers, such as the authors of the Upanishads and the Buddha, contributed to this rich tapestry of early thought. The Upanishads delved into profound metaphysical questions, exploring the nature of consciousness, the self, and ultimate reality. The Buddha, on the other hand, focused on practical teachings for alleviating suffering and achieving enlightenment. His insights into the nature of desire, attachment, and the path to liberation resonated with countless individuals and laid the foundation for Buddhism, which would spread across Asia and influence diverse cultures.

These ancient philosophical traditions, while diverse in their approaches and conclusions, shared a common goal: to uncover the fundamental truths of existence and provide guidance for living a meaningful life. They established the intellectual foundations upon which later thinkers would build, and their insights continue to resonate in contemporary discussions on ethics, science, and technology. As we explore the contributions of these early philosophers, we gain a deeper appreciation for the timeless quest for wisdom that has driven humanity forward and the ways in which their ideas have paved the way for technological advancement.

Would you like me to continue with the remaining chapters? Or do you have any specific preferences or adjustments you'd like to make?

continue automatically

Sure, I'll continue with the next chapters.

3

Chapter 3: Renaissance Rebirth: The Age of Enlightenment

The Renaissance period marked a significant turning point in the history of philosophy and technology. Emerging from the shadows of the Middle Ages, this era was characterized by a renewed interest in classical learning, humanism, and scientific inquiry. Philosophers and scholars of the Renaissance sought to reconcile the wisdom of ancient Greece and Rome with contemporary thought, leading to groundbreaking advancements in art, science, and technology. This intellectual revival laid the groundwork for the Enlightenment, a period of profound philosophical and technological innovation.

Key figures of the Renaissance, such as Leonardo da Vinci, embodied the intersection of philosophy and technology. Da Vinci's notebooks, filled with sketches of inventions, anatomical studies, and philosophical musings, showcased his multifaceted genius. His approach to understanding the natural world through observation and experimentation paved the way for future scientists and engineers. Similarly, the works of Galileo Galilei, who championed the scientific method and made significant contributions to astronomy and physics, exemplified the fusion of philosophical inquiry and technological innovation.

The Age of Enlightenment, which followed the Renaissance, further expanded the boundaries of human knowledge and understanding. Enlightenment philosophers, such as John Locke, Voltaire, and Immanuel Kant, emphasized reason, individualism, and empirical evidence as the foundations of knowledge. Their ideas challenged traditional authority and inspired new ways of thinking about society, politics, and ethics. Technological advancements during this period, including the development of the printing press and improvements in transportation, facilitated the widespread dissemination of these revolutionary ideas.

The Renaissance and Enlightenment periods were crucial in shaping the modern world. The intellectual curiosity and critical thinking that characterized these eras led to significant advancements in both philosophy and technology. The synergy between these fields not only transformed the way humans understood the world but also laid the foundation for the rapid technological progress that would follow in the centuries to come. By examining the contributions of these pivotal periods, we gain a deeper appreciation for the enduring relationship between philosophical thought and technological innovation.

4

Chapter 4: Industrial Revolution: The Steam-Powered Paradigm Shift

The Industrial Revolution marked a dramatic shift in the trajectory of human civilization. Beginning in the late 18th century, this period was characterized by rapid advancements in technology, industry, and urbanization. The introduction of steam power, mechanized manufacturing, and improved transportation systems revolutionized the way people lived and worked. This era of unprecedented technological progress had profound implications for philosophy, as thinkers grappled with the ethical and societal challenges posed by industrialization.

One of the most significant technological innovations of the Industrial Revolution was the steam engine, which enabled the mechanization of production and the expansion of transportation networks. Inventors like James Watt and George Stephenson played pivotal roles in refining and implementing this technology. The widespread adoption of steam power transformed industries such as textiles, mining, and transportation, leading to increased productivity and economic growth. However, this rapid industrialization also brought about social and environmental challenges, prompting philosophical debates on the ethics of progress and the impact of technology on human life.

Philosophers and social theorists of the Industrial Revolution, such as

Karl Marx and Friedrich Engels, critically examined the consequences of industrialization. In their seminal work, "The Communist Manifesto," they argued that the capitalist mode of production exploited workers and created significant economic inequalities. Their critique of industrial society highlighted the need for a more just and equitable system, and their ideas would go on to inspire various social and political movements. Other thinkers, such as John Stuart Mill, explored the balance between individual freedom and societal progress, advocating for reforms to address the negative effects of industrialization.

The Industrial Revolution underscored the complex relationship between technology and society. While technological advancements brought about unprecedented economic growth and improved living standards, they also raised important ethical and philosophical questions. The debates that emerged during this period continue to resonate in contemporary discussions on the role of technology in shaping human life. By understanding the philosophical and technological developments of the Industrial Revolution, we gain valuable insights into the ongoing dialogue between progress and ethics.

5

Chapter 5: Early Twentieth Century: Technological Genesis

The early twentieth century was a time of remarkable technological innovation and philosophical reflection. As the world entered the modern era, new inventions and discoveries transformed daily life and reshaped societal norms. The rapid pace of technological change prompted philosophers to reconsider traditional notions of reality, knowledge, and ethics. This period of intellectual and technological ferment set the stage for the dramatic developments that would characterize the remainder of the century.

The advent of electricity and the rise of mass communication were among the most significant technological advancements of the early twentieth century. Inventors like Thomas Edison and Nikola Tesla made groundbreaking contributions to the development of electrical power and wireless communication, revolutionizing the way people lived and interacted. The widespread adoption of these technologies facilitated the growth of new industries and the emergence of a truly interconnected global society. These innovations also raised important philosophical questions about the nature of progress and the ethical implications of technological advancement.

The early twentieth century also witnessed significant advancements in transportation, with the invention of the automobile and the airplane.

Pioneers like Henry Ford and the Wright brothers played crucial roles in developing and popularizing these new modes of transportation. The increased mobility afforded by these innovations had profound effects on society, shaping patterns of urbanization, commerce, and cultural exchange. Philosophers and social theorists grappled with the implications of these changes, exploring the ways in which technology influenced human behavior and societal structures.

The early twentieth century was a period of intense philosophical exploration, as thinkers sought to understand the rapidly changing world around them. Figures like Bertrand Russell, Martin Heidegger, and Ludwig Wittgenstein made significant contributions to the fields of logic, metaphysics, and language. Their work laid the foundation for many of the philosophical debates that would dominate the latter half of the century. By examining the technological and philosophical developments of the early twentieth century, we gain a deeper appreciation for the ways in which these two domains have shaped the modern world.

6

Chapter 6: The Digital Frontier: Silicon Valley and Beyond

The latter half of the twentieth century saw the rise of the digital age, driven by rapid advancements in computing and information technology. The development of the microprocessor and the personal computer revolutionized the way people lived, worked, and communicated. Silicon Valley emerged as the epicenter of this technological transformation, with companies like Intel, Apple, and Microsoft leading the charge. This digital revolution brought about profound changes in society, raising new philosophical questions about the nature of reality, identity, and knowledge in the digital age.

The advent of the internet further accelerated the pace of technological change, creating a global network that connected people and information like never before. The World Wide Web, developed by Tim Berners-Lee, transformed the internet from a niche technology into a ubiquitous platform for communication, commerce, and culture. The rise of social media platforms, such as Facebook, Twitter, and Instagram, further reshaped the way people interacted and shared information. These developments raised important philosophical questions about the implications of digital technology on privacy, identity, and the nature of human connection.

The digital age also saw the emergence of new philosophical movements, such as transhumanism, which advocates for the use of technology to enhance human capabilities and transcend biological limitations. Figures like Ray Kurzweil and Nick Bostrom have explored the potential benefits and risks of advanced technologies, such as artificial intelligence, genetic engineering, and nanotechnology. Their work has sparked debates about the ethical implications of technological enhancement and the future of humanity in a world increasingly shaped by digital technologies.

The digital frontier has brought about unprecedented opportunities and challenges, transforming virtually every aspect of human life. As we continue to navigate this rapidly changing landscape, it is essential to engage in thoughtful philosophical inquiry to understand the implications of these technologies and ensure that they are used to promote human flourishing. By examining the interplay between philosophy and technology in the digital age, we can gain valuable insights into the future of our increasingly interconnected and technologically advanced world.

7

Chapter 7: Artificial Intelligence: Conscious Machines?

The development of artificial intelligence (AI) represents one of the most significant technological advancements of the twenty-first century. From machine learning algorithms to autonomous robots, AI has the potential to revolutionize a wide range of industries and reshape the way we live and work. This technological breakthrough has also raised profound philosophical questions about the nature of consciousness, intelligence, and the ethical implications of creating machines that can think and learn.

Philosophers and scientists have long debated the nature of consciousness and whether it can be replicated in machines. The Turing Test, proposed by Alan Turing in 1950, is one of the earliest and most well-known attempts to define and measure artificial intelligence. According to Turing, a machine can be considered intelligent if it can engage in a conversation with a human and be indistinguishable from a human interlocutor. While AI systems have made significant progress in recent years, the question of whether they possess true consciousness or merely simulate intelligent behavior remains a topic of intense debate.

The ethical implications of AI are another critical area of philosophical inquiry. As AI systems become more advanced and integrated into various aspects of society, questions about accountability, fairness, and transparency become increasingly important. Issues such as algorithmic bias, data privacy, and the potential for job displacement require careful consideration to ensure that the benefits of AI are realized while minimizing potential harms. Philosophers, ethicists, and policymakers must work together to develop guidelines and regulations that address these concerns and promote the responsible development and use of AI.

The potential for AI to surpass human intelligence, known as the singularity, is a topic of both excitement and apprehension. Proponents of the singularity, such as Ray Kurzweil, argue that advanced AI could lead to unprecedented technological and societal advancements. However, others caution that the creation of superintelligent machines could pose significant risks to humanity, including the potential loss of control over these powerful systems. As we continue to explore the possibilities of artificial intelligence, it is essential to engage in thoughtful philosophical inquiry to understand the implications of these technologies and ensure that they are used to promote human flourishing.

8

Chapter 8: Cyber Ethics: Technology and Morality

The rapid advancement of technology has brought about new ethical challenges that require careful consideration and thoughtful dialogue. Cyber ethics, the study of ethical issues related to the use of digital technologies, has become an increasingly important field as technology continues to permeate every aspect of human life. From data privacy and cybersecurity to the ethical use of artificial intelligence, cyber ethics seeks to address the complex moral questions that arise in the digital age.

One of the most pressing ethical issues in the digital age is data privacy. The widespread collection and use of personal data by companies, governments, and other organizations raise important questions about consent, ownership, and the potential for misuse. Philosophers and ethicists have explored the implications of data privacy, advocating for stronger protections and regulations to ensure that individuals' rights are respected in an increasingly interconnected world. The balance between security and privacy is a central concern, as technological advancements make it easier to collect and analyze vast amounts of data.

Cybersecurity is another critical area of concern in the realm of cyber ethics. As digital technologies become more integral to our daily lives, the potential for cyberattacks and other malicious activities increases. The ethical implications of cybersecurity practices, such as surveillance, hacking, and digital warfare, require careful consideration to ensure that the rights and freedoms of individuals are protected while maintaining the security of digital systems. Philosophers and ethicists must grapple with the challenges posed by cybersecurity to develop guidelines and frameworks that promote ethical behavior in the digital age.

The ethical use of artificial intelligence is a particularly complex and multifaceted issue. As AI systems become more advanced and integrated into various aspects of society, questions about accountability, fairness, and transparency become increasingly important. Issues such as algorithmic bias, data privacy, and the potential for job displacement require careful consideration to ensure that the benefits of AI are realized while minimizing potential harms. Philosophers, ethicists, and policymakers must work together to develop guidelines and regulations that address these concerns and promote the responsible development and use of AI.

9

Chapter 9: The Knowledge Paradox: Information Overload

The digital age has brought about an unprecedented explosion of information. With the advent of the internet and the proliferation of digital devices, people have access to a vast array of information at their fingertips. While this abundance of information has the potential to empower individuals and enhance their knowledge, it also presents challenges related to information overload. The sheer volume of data available can make it difficult to discern accurate and relevant information, leading to a paradox where greater access to information does not necessarily result in greater understanding.

Philosophers and cognitive scientists have long explored the implications of information overload on human cognition and decision-making. The concept of "information fatigue syndrome" highlights the psychological and cognitive strain that can result from excessive exposure to information. As individuals are bombarded with a constant stream of news, social media updates, and digital content, they may struggle to process and retain meaningful information. This phenomenon raises important questions about the ways in which technology influences human cognition and the strategies that can be employed to manage information overload.

The challenge of information overload has also led to the development of new tools and technologies designed to help individuals navigate the digital landscape. Algorithms and artificial intelligence are increasingly used to filter and prioritize information, tailoring content to individual preferences and needs. While these technologies offer potential solutions to the problem of information overload, they also raise ethical concerns related to privacy, algorithmic bias, and the potential for manipulation. Philosophers and ethicists must grapple with these issues to ensure that the benefits of these technologies are realized while minimizing potential harms.

The knowledge paradox highlights the complex relationship between technology and human understanding. While digital technologies have the potential to democratize access to information and enhance individual knowledge, they also present significant challenges related to information overload and cognitive strain. By examining the philosophical and technological dimensions of this paradox, we can gain valuable insights into the ways in which technology shapes human cognition and the strategies that can be employed to promote meaningful engagement with information.

10

Chapter 10: Modern Philosophy: Reinterpreting Classical Thoughts

The rapid advancements in technology and the changing landscape of the modern world have prompted philosophers to revisit and reinterpret classical philosophical ideas. The timeless questions posed by ancient philosophers, such as the nature of reality, ethics, and the human condition, continue to resonate in contemporary discussions. Modern philosophers seek to bridge the gap between classical thought and the challenges of the digital age, offering new perspectives on age-old questions.

One area of focus for modern philosophers is the impact of technology on human identity and selfhood. The digital age has introduced new ways of understanding and expressing identity, from social media profiles to virtual realities. Philosophers like Michel Foucault and Judith Butler have explored the ways in which technology shapes and constructs identity, challenging traditional notions of the self. Their work highlights the fluid and dynamic nature of identity in the digital age, raising important questions about authenticity, agency, and the impact of technology on human relationships.

Modern philosophers also grapple with the ethical implications of technological advancements. The development of artificial intelligence, genetic engineering, and other emerging technologies raises complex moral questions that require careful consideration. Philosophers like Peter Singer and Martha

Nussbaum have examined the ethical dimensions of these technologies, advocating for principles such as utilitarianism and capabilities approach to guide ethical decision-making. Their work underscores the importance of ethical reflection in the development and use of technology.

    The reinterpretation of classical philosophical ideas in the context of modern technology offers valuable insights into the ways in which technology shapes human life and understanding. By engaging with the timeless questions posed by ancient philosophers, modern thinkers can develop new perspectives that address the unique challenges of the digital age. This ongoing dialogue between classical and contemporary thought enriches our understanding of the intersection of philosophy and technology, offering guidance for navigating the complexities of the modern world.

11

Chapter 11: Technological Determinism: Shaping Society

Technological determinism is a theory that posits that technology is the primary driver of societal change. According to this view, technological advancements shape the structure and values of society, influencing everything from economic systems to cultural norms. Proponents of technological determinism argue that the development and adoption of new technologies have far-reaching implications for human behavior and social organization.

The theory of technological determinism has been both supported and criticized by philosophers and social theorists. Figures like Marshall McLuhan and Alvin Toffler have argued that technology plays a central role in shaping human society, with McLuhan famously stating that "the medium is the message." Their work suggests that the ways in which information is communicated and consumed have a profound impact on societal values and behaviors. Critics of technological determinism, however, argue that this view overlooks the complex interplay between technology, culture, and human agency. They contend that while technology influences society, it is also shaped by social, political, and economic forces.

The impact of technological determinism can be seen in various aspects of modern life, from the rise of digital communication to the automation of labor.

The proliferation of digital technologies has transformed the way people interact, work, and access information, leading to significant changes in social and economic structures. The automation of labor, driven by advancements in robotics and artificial intelligence, has raised important questions about the future of work and the implications for economic inequality. These developments highlight the ways in which technology shapes society and the need for thoughtful reflection on the consequences of technological change.

The theory of technological determinism offers valuable insights into the relationship between technology and society, but it also underscores the importance of human agency and ethical reflection. While technology has the potential to drive significant societal change, it is essential to consider the broader social, political, and economic contexts in which technological advancements occur. By examining the complex interplay between technology and society, we can develop a more nuanced understanding of the ways in which technological determinism shapes the modern world.

12

Chapter 12: Future Visions: The Singularity

The concept of the singularity, a hypothetical point in the future when technological growth becomes uncontrollable and irreversible, has captured the imagination of futurists and technologists alike. Proponents of the singularity, such as Ray Kurzweil, argue that advancements in artificial intelligence, nanotechnology, and biotechnology will lead to a future where human and machine intelligence converge. This vision of the future raises profound philosophical questions about the nature of consciousness, the limits of human potential, and the ethical implications of creating superintelligent machines.

The singularity represents a radical departure from the current trajectory of technological development, with the potential to transform virtually every aspect of human life. Proponents of the singularity envision a future where humans can transcend biological limitations through technological enhancement, achieving immortality and superintelligence. This vision of the future raises important ethical and philosophical questions about the implications of such advancements for individual identity, social structures, and the nature of human existence.

Critics of the singularity argue that the concept is based on speculative and overly optimistic assumptions about the pace and trajectory of technological development. They caution that the risks associated with creating superintelligent machines, such as the potential loss of control and unforeseen consequences, may outweigh the potential benefits. Philosophers and ethicists must grapple with these concerns to develop frameworks for assessing the risks and benefits of advanced technologies and guiding their responsible development.

The concept of the singularity offers a thought-provoking vision of the future that challenges our understanding of technology, consciousness, and the limits of human potential. By exploring the philosophical and ethical dimensions of the singularity, we can gain valuable insights into the implications of advanced technologies and the ways in which they may shape the future of humanity. This ongoing dialogue between futurists, technologists, and philosophers is essential for navigating the complexities of a rapidly changing technological landscape and ensuring that the potential benefits of the singularity are realized while minimizing potential harms.

13

Chapter 13: Augmented Reality: Blending Realms

Augmented Reality (AR) represents a significant technological innovation that has the potential to transform the way we interact with the world. Unlike virtual reality, which creates entirely digital environments, AR overlays digital information onto the physical world, enhancing our perception of reality. This blending of realms raises intriguing philosophical questions about the nature of reality, perception, and the relationship between the digital and physical worlds.

The development of AR technologies, such as Microsoft's HoloLens and Google's ARCore, has opened up new possibilities for education, entertainment, and industry. For example, AR can be used to create immersive educational experiences, allowing students to interact with historical events or explore complex scientific concepts in a more engaging and interactive way. In the realm of entertainment, AR has the potential to create new forms of storytelling and gaming that merge the physical and digital worlds. These applications of AR raise important questions about the ways in which technology can enhance and transform human experiences.

Philosophers and ethicists have also explored the implications of AR for concepts such as presence and identity. The ability to overlay digital information onto the physical world challenges traditional notions of presence and raises questions about the boundaries between the real and the virtual. As individuals navigate these blended environments, they may also encounter new challenges related to privacy, consent, and the ethical use of digital information. Philosophers must grapple with these issues to develop frameworks for understanding and addressing the ethical implications of AR.

The blending of realms facilitated by AR offers exciting possibilities for enhancing human experiences and interactions. However, it also presents significant philosophical and ethical challenges that require careful consideration. By exploring the ways in which AR transforms our perception of reality and examining the ethical implications of these technologies, we can develop a deeper understanding of the ways in which technology shapes human life and experience. This ongoing dialogue between philosophers, technologists, and ethicists is essential for navigating the complexities of the digital age and ensuring that AR is used to promote human flourishing.

14

Chapter 14: Sustainable Tech: Green Philosophies

As the world grapples with the challenges of climate change and environmental degradation, the development of sustainable technologies has become a critical area of focus. Green technologies, such as renewable energy, electric vehicles, and sustainable agriculture, aim to reduce the environmental impact of human activities and promote a more sustainable future. This shift towards sustainability raises important philosophical questions about our relationship with the environment and the ethical implications of technological advancement.

The philosophy of environmental ethics explores the moral principles that guide our interactions with the natural world. Thinkers like Aldo Leopold and Arne Næss have argued for a more harmonious and respectful relationship with the environment, advocating for principles such as deep ecology and the land ethic. These philosophical perspectives emphasize the intrinsic value of nature and the importance of preserving ecological systems for future generations. The development of sustainable technologies aligns with these principles, offering new ways to mitigate the impact of human activities on the environment.

Sustainable technologies also raise important questions about the balance between economic development and environmental preservation. The transition to renewable energy sources, such as solar and wind power, has the potential to reduce greenhouse gas emissions and promote energy independence. However, this transition also requires significant investments and changes to existing infrastructure. Philosophers and ethicists must grapple with the trade-offs and challenges associated with sustainable development, exploring ways to balance economic growth with environmental stewardship.

The pursuit of sustainable technologies represents a critical intersection of philosophy and technology, offering new ways to address the pressing environmental challenges of our time. By examining the ethical and philosophical dimensions of sustainability, we can develop a deeper understanding of the principles that guide our interactions with the environment and the ways in which technology can be harnessed to promote a more sustainable future. This ongoing dialogue between philosophers, technologists, and policymakers is essential for developing solutions that promote both human and environmental flourishing.

15

Chapter 15: Conclusion: The Ever-Evolving Intersection

Throughout this exploration of the intersection between philosophy and technology, we have seen how these two domains have influenced and shaped each other throughout history. From the earliest days of human civilization to the digital age, philosophical inquiry and technological innovation have driven humanity forward, offering new ways to understand and interact with the world. This dynamic interplay has resulted in profound advancements and raised important ethical and philosophical questions that continue to resonate today.

As we look to the future, the relationship between philosophy and technology will only become more critical. The rapid pace of technological change presents both exciting opportunities and significant challenges, requiring thoughtful reflection and ethical consideration. Philosophers, technologists, and ethicists must work together to navigate the complexities of the digital age, ensuring that technological advancements are harnessed to promote human flourishing and address the pressing challenges of our time.

The ever-evolving intersection of philosophy and technology offers valuable insights into the ways in which these two domains can complement and enhance each other. By engaging in thoughtful philosophical inquiry and ethical reflection, we can develop a deeper understanding of the implications of technological advancements and the principles that should guide their development and use. This ongoing dialogue is essential for navigating the complexities of the modern world and shaping a future that promotes both human and environmental well-being.

In conclusion, the relationship between philosophy and technology is a testament to the power of human thought and ingenuity. By examining the ways in which these two domains have intersected and influenced each other throughout history, we gain a deeper appreciation for the ways in which they have shaped our world and our understanding of it. As we move forward into an increasingly technologically advanced future, it is essential to continue this dialogue, fostering a thoughtful and ethical approach to technological innovation that promotes the well-being of all.

Description: In "The Philosopher's Code: Unlocking the Intersection of History and Technology," embark on a compelling journey through time as the profound interplay between philosophical thought and technological innovation unfolds. This captivating exploration delves into the pivotal moments where these two domains have intersected, from the ancient wisdom of philosophers like Socrates and Confucius to the cutting-edge advancements of Silicon Valley.

Discover how the Renaissance and the Industrial Revolution reshaped human understanding and societal structures, leading to the rapid technological genesis of the early twentieth century. Examine the digital frontier and the rise of artificial intelligence, uncovering the ethical dilemmas and philosophical debates that these advancements provoke.

Engage with contemporary discussions on cyber ethics, the knowledge paradox, and the reinterpretation of classical philosophical ideas in the context of modern technology. Delve into the theory of technological determinism and the futuristic visions of the singularity, augmented reality, and sustainable tech, all while contemplating the ever-evolving relationship between technology and society.

With each chapter, "The Philosopher's Code" invites readers to ponder the timeless questions of existence, identity, and morality, offering insights into how we can harness the power of both philosophy and technology to shape a

CHAPTER 15: CONCLUSION: THE EVER-EVOLVING INTERSECTION

better world. This thought-provoking book serves as a guide to navigating the complexities of our technologically advanced future, providing a deeper understanding of the intersection of history and innovation.

www.ingramcontent.com/pod-product-compliance
Lightning Source LLC
LaVergne TN
LVHW020503080526
838202LV00057B/6127